To: _____

From: _____

Published by Cumberland House Publishing, an imprint of Sourcebooks, Inc.
P.O. Box 4410, Naperville, Illinois 60567–4410
(630) 961–3900
Fax: (630) 961–2168
www.sourcebooks.com

Printed and bound in China
OGP 10 9 8 7 6 5 4

Why A Daughter Needs A Mom

Coupons

GREGORY E. LANG

CUMBERLAND HOUSE

A daughter needs a mom

to provide her with memories that will last forever.

Good for an evening of looking through photo albums and reminiscing together.

A daughter needs a mom

to teach her not to let a good day slip from her fingers.

Rainy Day Coupon: Even though it's dreary outside, let's make hot cocoa and watch your favorite movie.

A daughter needs a mom
to teach her how to cook.

Let's test my skills—I'll make dinner tonight.

A daughter needs a mom

to tell her that beauty never fades if you look in the right places.

You taught me to appreciate the beauty in so many things.
Let's spend a day together in the garden.

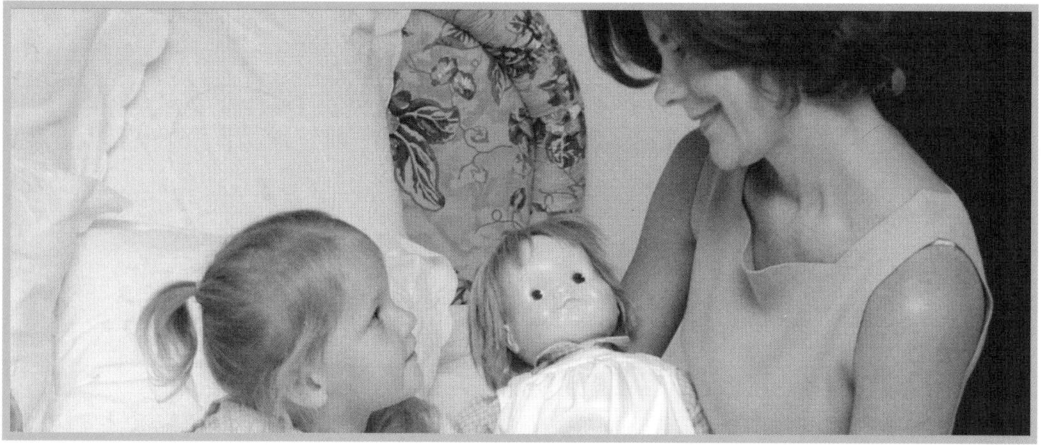

A daughter needs a mom

who can play on her level.

Let's go to the park and play on the swings together just like we used to.

A daughter needs a mom

to show her how to give back to others.

I'd like to do something for you: This coupon is good for breakfast in bed.

A daughter needs a mom

to show her how to use humor to lighten heavy loads.

This coupon is good for a day of laughter.
Let's go out and act crazy for awhile!

A daughter needs a mom

who knows how to let loose and have fun.

Free Weekend Coupon: Good for a weekend free of chores or responsibilities.

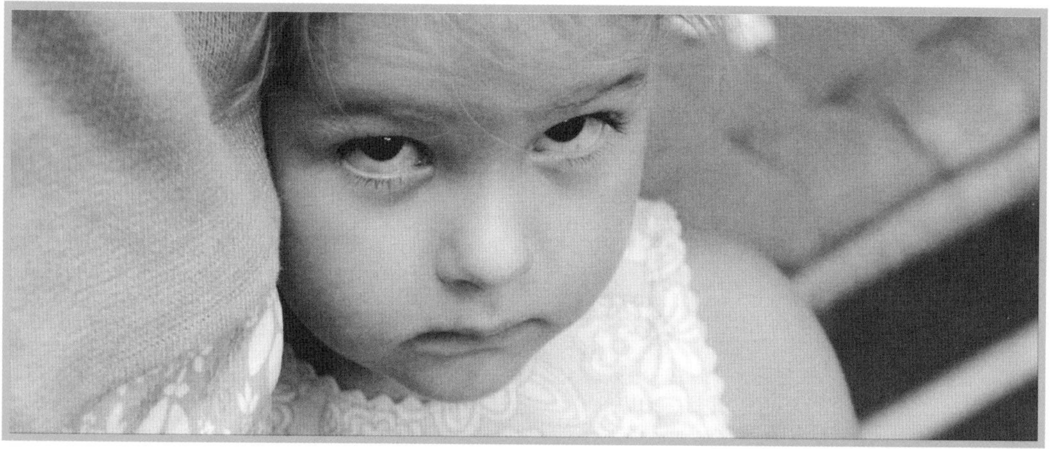

A daughter needs a mom

to remind her, on the bad days, that she is not alone.

Mom, let's go somewhere we both love—just the two of us.

A daughter needs a mom

to remind her to save some time and
energy for herself.

This coupon reminds you to do the same. Good for one
uninterrupted bubble-bath hour.

A daughter needs a mom

to teach her that the path taken means as much
as the destination.

Mom, you choose the trail this weekend—let's go for a walk or hike together.

A daughter needs a mom

to indulge her individuality.

This coupon entitles you to a bouquet of your very favorite flowers.

A daughter needs a mom

to teach her that her body is a temple.

This coupon is redeemable for a morning of relaxation and revitalization.

A daughter needs a mom

to give her the freedom to express herself.

Dancing Queen Coupon: Mom, let's put on your favorite tunes and dance!

A daughter needs a mom

to show her the comfort of a warm embrace.

Good for a big hug whenever you need it.

A daughter needs a mom

to carry her when she is tired.

It's my turn. I'll do the dishes tonight—you deserve a break.

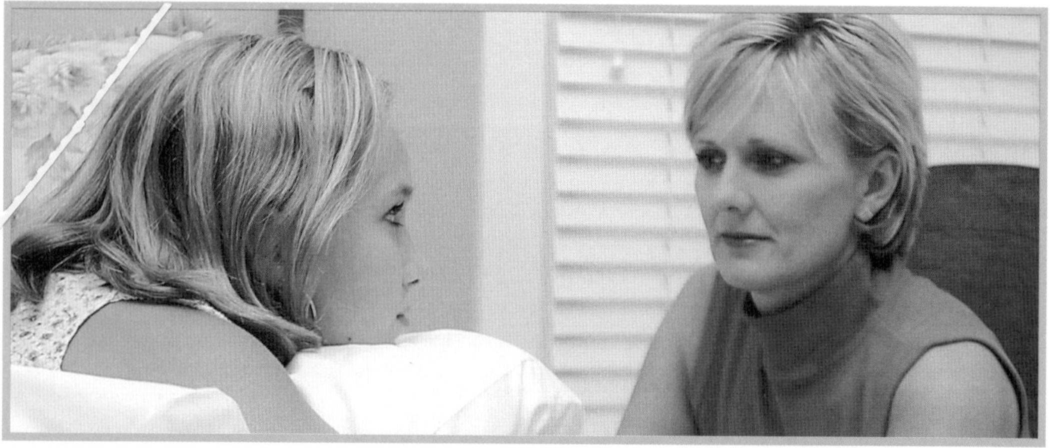

A daughter needs a mom

to teach her the art of conversation.

Let's practice! Good for chitchat and a tea party for two.

A daughter needs a mom

who will sing along with her when her favorite song comes on the radio.

Let's go for a ride—you pick the radio station and we'll practice our skills!

A daughter needs a mom

to remind her that she has the right to
indulge herself now and then.

Mom, let's get your favorite chocolate and enjoy it together.

A daughter needs a mom

who believes it is okay to see things differently.

This time, you get the last word: Good for winning one argument, no contest.

A daughter needs a mom

to remind her to be playful, no matter how old she is.

Girls Night Out: Mom, call your girlfriends and go out on the town!

A daughter needs a mom
to tell her not to be afraid to seize the moment.

Mom, you've taught me to see potential in every circumstance, even a rainy day.
Let's enjoy a peaceful walk in the rain together.